# The Wisdom of Women

10 Decades.
10 Women.
5 Questions.

Deborah Monk

LifePondering Press
deb@deborahmonk.com



The Wisdom of Women / Deborah Monk. -- 1st ed.
ISBN 978-1-7323384-4-9

*This book is dedicated to all the women and girls brave enough to ask questions...and daring enough to answer them.*

# Contents

*Aging is the vehicle that allows us to travel through the stages of womanhood. Fasten your seatbelt and enjoy the ride, because resisting aging denies you the incredible beauty of every age, every transformation that is what it means to be a woman.*

# My 20's

When I was in my twenties, this is the advice I got about aging from my mother.

"There will come a day," my mother said, "when you will walk into a room, and they won't notice you."

I wondered who they were and why they mattered so much.

"You will feel invisible," she whispered with a touch of venom, "and you won't like it."

I felt guilty, somehow responsible for her jealousy. I wanted to tell her they weren't noticing me, they were just seeing young and shiny. And sure, I'll admit I enjoyed being noticed, but it also took effort. It required figuring out what they wanted and then contorting myself to fit inside that box. It was fun, but I wouldn't want to do it forever.

Not being noticed sounded freeing. A chance to be whomever I wanted.

If I had a daughter one day, I hoped I wouldn't ask her to dim her light because of my own desperate need to still be noticed. I hoped I would gracefully slip into the shadows and enjoy watching the world appreciate her young beauty.

I said a silent prayer that when I stopped being noticed, I would step into my own super-power of invisibility.

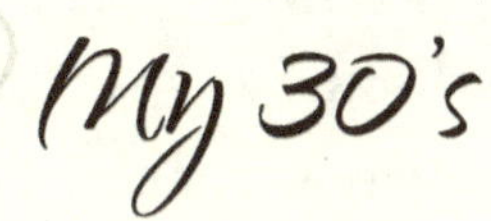

# My 30's

When I was in my thirties, this was the advice I got about aging from Jane Fonda.

In her book, My Life So Far, Ms. Fonda introduced me to the idea that aging could be like a play, with a first act, a second act, and a third act. I never thought of my life as having three acts, nor had I considered that the last act could be the best.

"Perhaps aging," she wrote, "should be a spiral staircase. Because the wisdom, balance, reflection and compassion that this upward movement represents doesn't just come in one linear ascension, that they circle around us, beckoning us to keep climbing, to keep looking both back and ahead."

I have never heard anyone speak of aging this way before. Ever. It sounds so radical that it must be crazy.

However, sometimes you just have to throw away the old road map to find your own way and this sounded like a much more desirable way to go through life.

Battle, peak, crash and burn. . .

or live a wonderful and wild third act that would make me want to jump to my feet with a standing ovation for my own life story?

*I'll take the later please.*

# My 40's

When I was in my forties, this was the advice I got about aging from a statue.

Browsing in a store, I found a wooden sculpture that spoke to my soul. Carved in dark wood, it was three women dancing side by side; a young woman, a pregnant woman, and a wise woman. I bought it and named it "The Trilogy of Womanhood."

I did some research and discovered the sculpture is more commonly known as "The Maiden, The Mother, and The Crone."

Maiden and Mother I understood. But Crone?

The dictionary defines Crone as, "a cru-el or ugly old woman." The woman on my statue wasn't cruel or ugly. She was as radiant as the other two.

I did more research.

Literature describes the Crone as a wise woman who embodies the instinctive way of channeling wisdom, inner knowing, and intuition. She is a guide through the transitions of life, and goes inward to bring forth the light of transformation.

*I want to be a Crone when I grow up.*

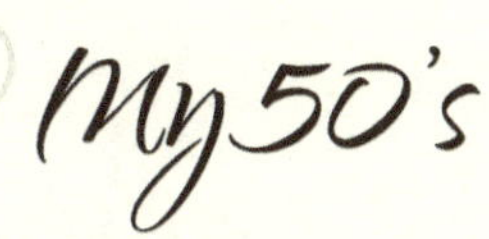

# My 50's

When I was in my fifties, this is the advice I got about aging from my mother.

"You should be afraid of aging," my mother warned me.

I reminded her that I was fifty-four, hardly a spring chicken.

"You just haven't gotten to the scary part," she spat out.

"So what age should I start being afraid?" I asked.

She looked at me and I swore she was adding a few years to my age. "Sixty." I could tell it was an arbitrary number.

I wanted to respect her opinion, but I couldn't sacrifice my own. "Aging doesn't frighten me," I whispered, not in defiance of her, but in deference to myself.

*The world, the media, and my family have told me that aging is a race against time that we are all destined to lose. Yet, the seeds of sacred wisdom I've gathered along the way have taken root in my soul. They dare me to face a truth so profound that it could turn our world upside down.*

# At 55

At fifty-five, I think aging is awesome.

If I had known this stage existed, that I would feel my own potential vibrating inside of me faster and stronger than it ever has before, I wouldn't have worried so much about getting older.

When I was little, people would ask what I wanted to be when I grew up. The right answer, the only answer I knew or ever heard, was go to college. Start a career. Get married. Have kids.

No one thinks beyond that. No one asks beyond that. No one ever told me there is a time, a space, a whole world after accomplishing those things.

Maybe in past generations there wasn't. And maybe even now, other people don't know it exists, just like I didn't.

What if...

aging means I get to ask myself that question again? What do I want to be when I grow up? Now that I've lived, and loved, and lost. Now that I know myself more fully. Maybe now is the first time I can really answer that question.

What if...

aging means we get to create our own personal playground, with the imagination of our childhood and the ability and assets of our adulthood?

What if...

aging is a chance to remove the cataracts of our soul? To strip ourselves of false identities? To take off the masks we've worn to keep everyone else comfortable?

So I want to believe what I know... that aging can be a playground.

And I'm equally terrified that I am wrong. Because my theory of aging goes against everything I've been told, everything I can see and hear and touch. So much so, that I wonder if I'm crazy. When the whole world is running out of a burning building, screaming, "Aging sucks!", how can I be running toward it, shouting, "This is awesome!"

There's only one reason to go back into a burning building.

There is something in there that you value more than your own life.

And the seed of the possibility that I am right, that my life is meant to be my own playground, makes it worth going back in. Because what's at stake is the rest of my life.

And when I lose my courage, my confidence, when I feel like it would be so much easier to go with the flow, with the status quo, when I'm petrified the scales of time will tip and I will succumb to the popular paradigm of aging, I remember there is something even more important at risk than my own future. . .

My daughter's future. My niece's future. The future of all the maidens and mothers who are looking to us crones to lead the charge. To forge the path. To illuminate and inhabit this new way of aging.

Armed with pen and paper, faith and fear, I am ready to run back into the burning building.

Maybe I'm crazy. Maybe I'm wrong.

But what if...

*What if aging can be awesome?*

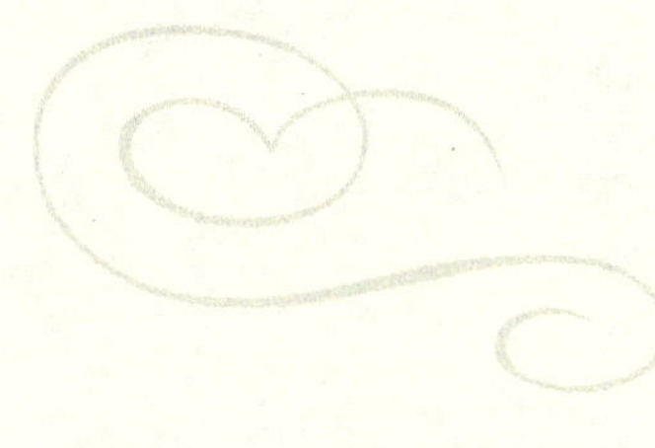

Chapter two

# Seryn

Born: Nashua, New Hampshire
10 Years Old

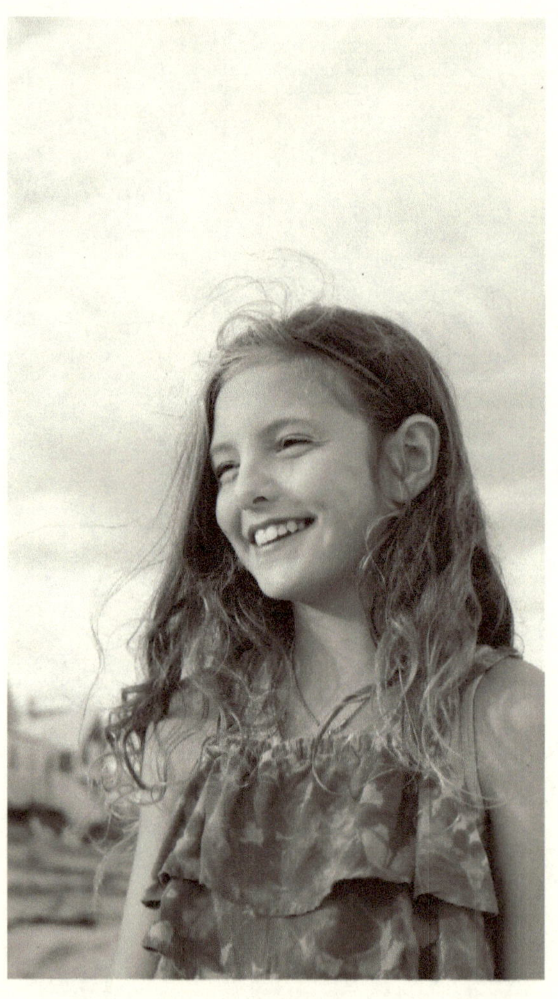

I met Seryn when I hired her mother to draw the cover for one of my handmade books. Seryn came to the door, peeking out from behind her mother. "I like your dress," she said to me. A girl complimenting a woman. A female admiring another female. A thought flittered briefly across my mind - Imagine if we started every conversation, every initial meeting, with a compliment.

I heard a distant whisper from the Universe...Maybe she should be in the wisdom of women book.

I quickly reminded myself, and the Universe, that I had decided a teenager would be the youngest person I would interview. Seryn was only ten years old. What could she possibly know about what it means to be woman?

A few weeks later, I went back to their house to pick up my book cover. Just in case Seryn was there, and to entertain her, I purposefully wore another dress, an evening gown that I had shortened.

Again, Seryn noticed and admired out loud. She was shy, but still strong enough to compliment a complete stranger.

Altogether, I had been in the presence of Seryn for a total of two minutes, yet I couldn't stop thinking about her after I left. It was like the Universe was shining a shimmering spotlight on her that only I could see. This time, I heard the whisper much stronger. Seryn needs to be in this book.

Never one to ignore my Muse's guidance, I called Seryn's mother and told her about this project.

We meet in a quaint little coffee shop. Her mother and brother sit at a table away from us so Seryn and I can sit by ourselves in a little nook with shabby chic chairs and a painted metal garden table by ourselves.

I am the author. The adult. The one in charge. I ask the first question.

Seryn moves like a butterfly. Her slender body is in constant flight as she talks, her arms and hands gentle wings that help her express her thoughts and emotions.

The ultimate maiden, she captivates me with her clarity, her vulnerability, and her inner knowing.

She reminds me I am still a girl in a woman's body.

And Seryn is already a woman in a girl's body.

I sit there, entranced. Watching her be so whole, so unbowed by expectations and the heartache of life, she sets me free as I follow her enchanted flight into the world of an old soul.

# 1 What would you tell your younger self?

Seryn points to a beauty mark on her face. I used to worry about this when I was younger. I would look in a mirror and say I can never look pretty with this on my face. My brother would say only witches have marks like this. It looks so ugly and it makes me ugly.

She smiles. If I could go back, I would look in the mirror and tell me not to say those things to myself. I would never talk to myself that way now.

# 2 What would you tell your older self?

No matter how old you are, you can't let what people say to you stop you. Things like, you're too old. You will feel the same way as you get older. Your body is the only thing that is getting older. Don't sit on the couch all day because you are afraid you'll hurt your back. Everything has risk. Would you rather die in a hospital or die doing something you love?

# 3 What is most important to you right now?

My biggest fear is I'll forget to say thank you. What if I have an argument with my Mom and she passes away?

My Mom tells me to treat everyone like it's their last day on earth.

When I was two, my mother had an argument with her mother. Then my Mom went away for the weekend with my Dad and me. That Saturday night, she called her Mom and said, "I'm sorry and I love you."

Her mother, my grandmother, said, "I was just going to call you. I am sorry and I love you, too!"

My grandmother died the next day.

# 4 What do you struggle to accept about yourself?

I'm changing a lot. Complete germaphobe. OCD. Everything has to be perfect. If I wash and dry my hands, and then touch a chair, I have to wash and dry my hands again.

Anxiety about school wrecked me. One night I was staying at Papa's and I had a panic attack. Mom came and slept over with me.

I'll never go to bars, always something horrifies me of bars. So many people hurt themselves that way. I'd rather pass away, because I don't want the people who love me to be disappointed that I had a choice and did it to myself.

# 5 What do you love about yourself?

I feel like I am older. Kids feel younger than me. I am able to understand stuff more simply. I am aware of so many more things than other kids my age.

My Mom shares and I am interested. She tells me the honest truth, not to scare me, but so I'll be less scared.

And Pop Pop gives me the newspaper. He cuts out scary stories.

*"Your soul never gets older."*

*Seryn*

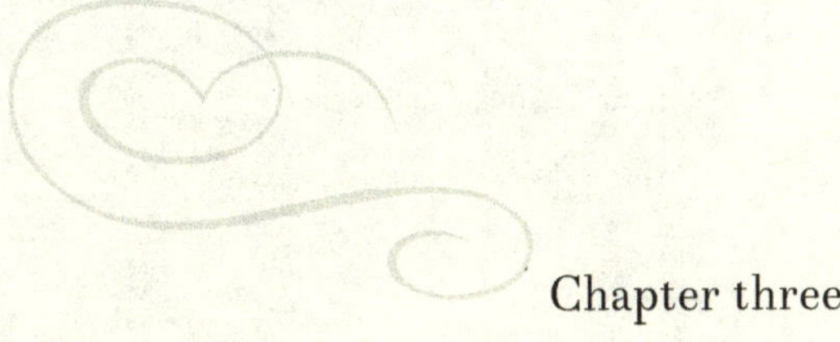

Chapter three

# Saige

Born: Derry, New Hampshire
20 Years Old

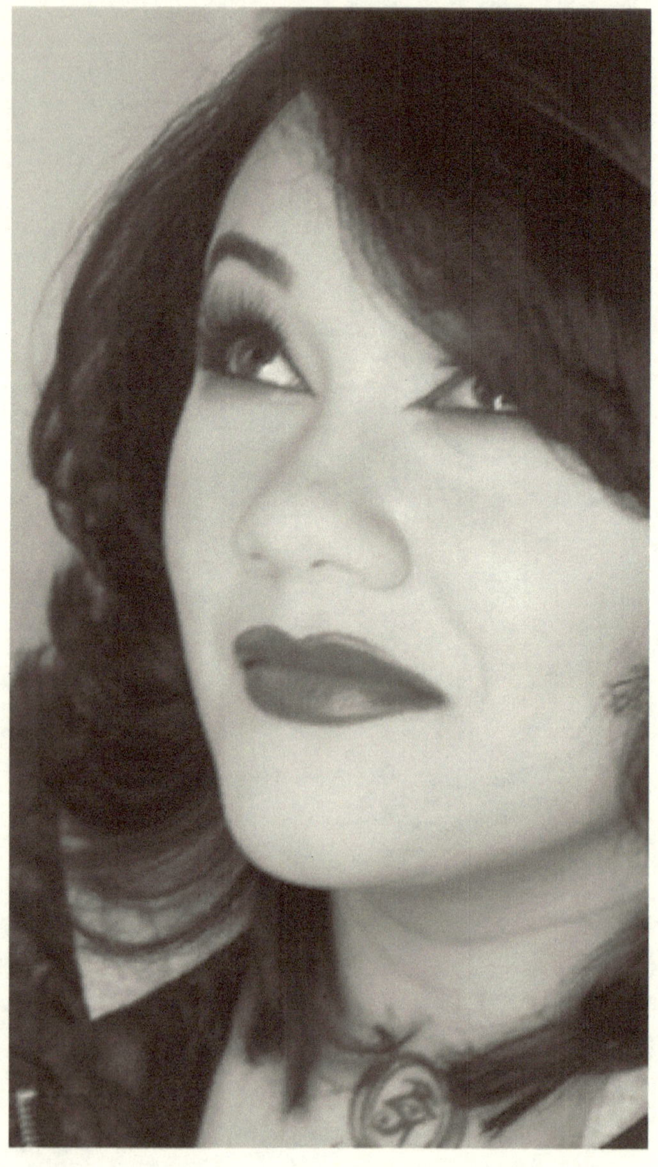

My dear friend Shelly is a national hair-stylist who does hair all over the United States. She recently became the Creative Director of a new company.

Whenever Shelly asks me to do something, I always say yes before she can even finish her sentence telling me what she's got up her magical sleeve. Because it's always fun. Always interesting. And most of the time, it's outside of my comfort zone.

This time, however, she wanted me to model. The yes died on my lips and I wished I could take it back. I reminded her I am not a model. She said, "That's perfect. My company wants "real" women."

I am reminded of a line from the "Velveteen Rabbit." Generally, by the time you are Real, most of your hair has been loved off, and your eyes drop off and you get loose in the joints and very shabby. But these things don't matter at all, because once you are Real, you can't be ugly, except to people who don't understand."

Okay, I guess I'm real.

When I arrive at the photo shoot, I am impressed by how professional everyone is. Professional photographer. Professional make-up artist. Professional stylist.

Except, of course, for me and two other real women.

Saige, the fourth "model", is running late because she has a three-month-old daughter. I am sitting in the make-up chair so I can't turn my head when I heard Saige arrive. Someone asks her what nationality she is.

"Egyptian, Jamaican, and Irish," she says.

Such an intriguing combination. Please, please, please, I pray, let her be in her twenties.

And she is.

With her dark mane of curls, her full lips and her soft voice, and that invisible shimmering spotlight shining on her, she becomes our perfect twenty-something-year-old woman.

# 1 What would you tell your younger self?

When I was thirteen years old, I was very depressed and sad. I didn't feel good enough or worthy of love and friendship. I was in my head, trying to force what I didn't have and focused on everything I thought I wasn't enough of. Somehow I knew I had to hold on and depend on myself to find the answers for life. Books introduced me to Buddhism and I loved it. When I was fourteen, I converted from Catholic to Buddhism. It was really hard. I lived with my mother, grandmother, and grandfather. My mother was supportive, but my grandmother had very hard blinders on. In her mind, you're Catholic.... or you are Catholic to her.

For me, it was the release I needed from sadness and pain. I finally released no matter what happen, life will always work out and I will always be okay.

# 2 What would you tell your older self?

I am really proud of you.

Chill out. Even more. Try to stop worrying and always trying to be ahead. Calm down, take your time, and enjoy the moment more than you already do.

By now you know that even crappy situations have a reason and a purpose. So go with the flow and continue to leave it up to your future self and everything will be alright.

# 3 What is most important to you right now?

My daughter. She's changed my perspective on life. Teaching her to be a good person is teaching myself at the same time. And she's teaching me patience

My husband. I met him at a swimming pond because I was dating his best friend. That first day I met him, my brain told me I was going to marry him someday. I thought I was going crazy. He is the first man who has treated me with any form of respect, compassion, and understanding.

My mother. I consider her my first love. She's my rock. She doesn't judge me and I know she is always there for me.

# 4 What do you struggle to accept about yourself?

I don't think I do, as crazy as that sounds. I try to let go of what isn't and what I don't have and accept what I do have and move forward.

When I was in my early teens, I struggled a lot with my body image. I thought looks had superior value and I didn't feel attractive. The Buddhist perception of the body is it's a vehicle for life. The body helps us move around and get things done. Beauty is temporary. In twenty or thirty years, if I am the worst looking person in the world, I will roll with those punches.

# 5 What do you love about yourself?

I love who I am.

It took me a while to accept myself.

Now that I know beauty is on the inside, I feel beautiful. And I don't believe in the possession of my own body because it's ever-changing.

*"Whether it's social media, or your own family, there will always be someone telling you that you are not enough. Ignore them. Be the best version of yourself and do what you love. Don't believe the comments because that is what will hurt you."*

*Saige*

Chapter four

# Maria

Born: Cincinnati, Ohio
33 Years Old

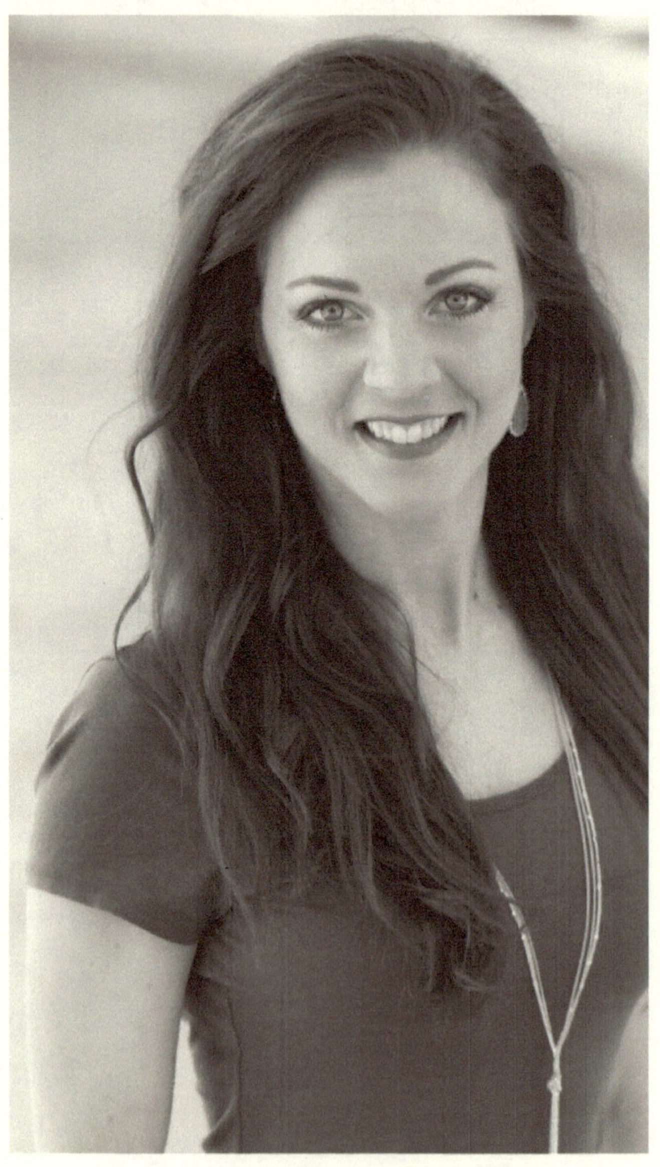

I have always found ballroom dancing to be the most beautiful blend of masculine and feminine energy. The epitome of independence and intimacy.

When I saw Maria and Alyenendrov dance, I saw the masculine and feminine energy in each of them, intertwining into an incomparable whole. They have that "it" factor.

So who better than this woman, this dancer, so strong and graceful and complete on her own, yet so connected and melded with her partner, to be our thirty-something-year-old.

When we meet, Maria folds her body on her chair like an origami ballerina. She wraps her hands around her hot cup of tea as she listens to my questions.

Her intention is that of a teacher

Her attention is that of a student.

I sense an integral relationship quality to Maria. She is in partnership with whomever she is engaged with. In relationship with the present. Like a grand plie, she sinks into this moment and takes me with her into a meditative contemplation of my questions.

# 1 What would you tell your younger self?

Stop being afraid sooner.

I grew up in a classic suburban household. We weren't rich, but I had a very happy childhood with a strong sense of security. The expectation was. . . this is how life goes. Not in an oppressive way, just a clearly marked road of life.

I became a math teacher with a comfortable, stable job. I felt this pull inside me to follow my heart but I was afraid to leave the security of what I knew.

Then I took a ballroom dance lesson from Alyenendrov and right from the start, he wanted me to be his professional partner. But I was afraid. So I did both, taught math all day and danced all night.

People often ask when and how did I finally say yes to my heart. And to him. It doesn't sound brave, by my answer is exhaustion. I did both as long as I could and I just couldn't do it anymore. So when I was too tired to be afraid, I said yes.

# 2 What would you tell your older self?

What I try to do now, and hope I will continue doing in the future, is to not forget what it felt like to be a specific age or in a certain situation.

I think it's easy to grow out of a stage and to look back, and to look down, on it...to think it isn't, or wasn't, a big deal.

Seeing others, and even myself, where I once was, makes me grateful for the reminder.

The more we can put ourselves in other's shoes and remember what it was like, the better stewards we can be.

# 3 What is most important to you right now?

At every age, it's to be the best me I can be.

In pursuit of that, at this point in my life, Alenendrov and I want to win Nationals and Blackpool, the two biggest dance competitions.

Alyenendrov is the most disciplined person I've ever met. He brings discipline and routine and actionable items to the table. And vulnerability and open-heartedness are my strengths. That is why we make good partners, in dance and in life, because I will learn from him and he can learn from me.

# 4 What do you struggle to accept about yourself?

I can't do or be everything.

As a teacher, sometimes I needed to be mother, father, disciplinarian, teacher, psychologist, and no matter how much I gave, it was never enough.

Because I have the ability or gift to see things that are lacking, see the things that are missing or aren't being nurtured, seeing what isn't there yet kills me.

My brain knows I can't do it all, be it all, but sometimes my heart doesn't and it causes me a lot of pain.

# 5 What do you love about yourself?

I am thankful I am well educated and intelligent. I like what that does for me. I think one of my talents is being able to look at situations and see what is missing, so I can help improve. Give me a seed of something and I will blow it up, make it grow to exceed your expectations. Give me a little and I will give you a lot back.

I look back on things and learn and grow. It's not fun to look back at sad times, at failures, when you got hurt or you hurt someone, but I like that I have the courage to do that and try to grow so I can prevent it from happening again. It's cathartic and healing. And by learning, I can reach out and touch someone else, maybe preventing or helping them through a similar type of pain.

I also love my personal relationship to God. I wouldn't have the wisdom, or the strength, or the courage; nothing I do or have would be possible without that support and love behind me.

*"I know a lot of old people who don't act old. And a lot of people who are not old in years, but are old in spirit. Aging is letting things stagnate and anything stagnant decreases in quality."*

*Maria*

Chapter five

# Hadiiya

Born: Brooklyn, New York
42 Years Old

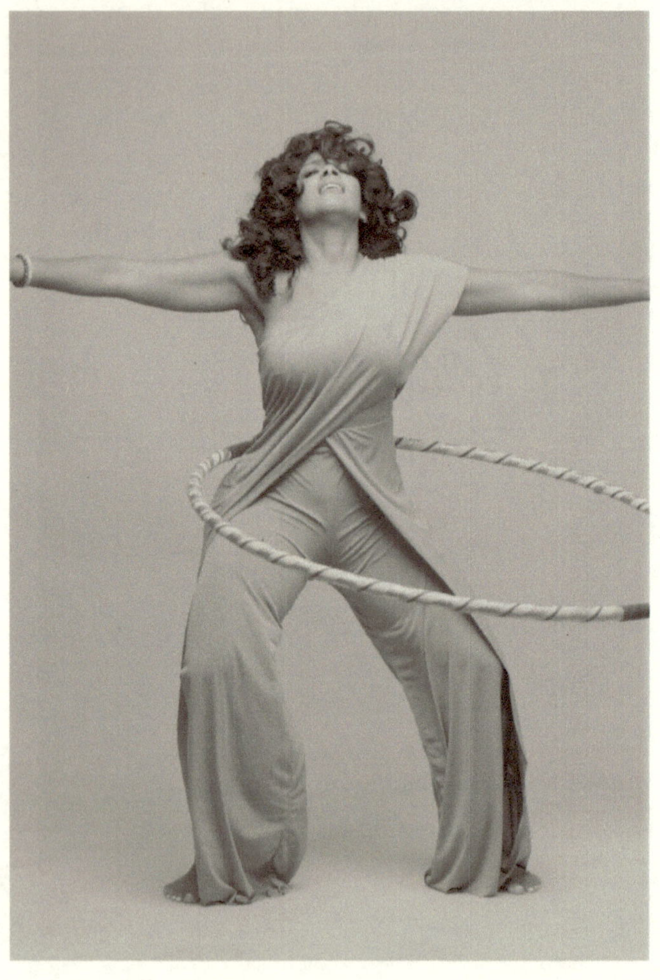

A friend of mine invited me to a book launch party in New York City. If I drive, she said, she'll pay for the hotel. And I should bring a Goddess dress. That's all I know as I pack my overnight bag.

This isn't your normal, conservative book launch. The author is a wig-maker to the stars and we are going to her shop in Brooklyn. The streets are tight, the traffic is jammed, and the three flights of stairs in the old brick building are congested where we wait in line to go inside.

The shop is relatively small and there's a lot going on, but it doesn't feel packed. Hadiiya created space for the launch of her first book, What If You Just Turned Your Magic All the Way the F*ck On. The walls are all white with big glass windows. There's a deejay against one wall and little booths selling hand-made items in the corners. Then Hadiiya pulls a hula hoop out and starts dancing in the middle of the room, swinging the hula around to the beat of the music. Hadiiya has the joy of a five-year-old, but the undulating her hips of a woman who has loved. Who has known life and given birth. Soon, she takes it off and passes it to another woman who takes center stage.

When it's my turn, I accept the hula hoop. I haven't hula'd in decades. Don't know if I remember how.

I look over at Hadiiya. Her spirit and energy take up a lot of room, but instead of making me feel small; she embraces me with her energy and fills me. She is like a human permission slip to be bigger and bolder and more glorious that I ever imagined I could be.

I step into the hula and dance.

# 1 What would you tell your younger self?

You've been waiting your whole life to get the perfect boobs. You will get them.

You will enjoy them. You will play a voluptuous character and play it well.

Then you will wish you never had them.

And I will take care of you.

There is a whole other world waiting for you. There's no need to rush.

Learn more about the things that make you unique and special and use those to see your beauty, rather than seeing what you think you are lacking.

Take your time to love.

Let them court you.

# 2 What would you tell your older self?

I'm coming! I'm breaking these chains and inching my way to you. I can hear you now. I can feel your energy pulling me toward you, and I'm no longer afraid of all perceived bondages, restraints and constraints. I can't wait to melt in your embrace.

And I can hear her, my spirit self, my old self, responding back... "Girl, it took you a while to get it together. I've been admiring you from afar, waiting, and knowing you would find your way to me. Keep coming. Enjoy this time and have all the experiences you can, all of it, don't hold back. Let it free. Let it shine.

This is your time!

# 3 What is most important to you right now?

A strong foundation.

A life foundation.

A solid financial foundation so I can do what I love and not worry about money.

I want no separation between being a professional... and being a priestess!

I want to embrace yay sexuality, my power point, my creative source, and use it for everything!

# 4 What do you struggle to accept about yourself?

I am always late. I'm a little scattered. I like to do too much and wish I could be more focused. I want to do everything. It's a daily struggle. Why can't I clean just one room, instead of cleaning a little bit in four rooms?

I'm trying to accept some of this so life will be an easier experience.

I wish I wasn't so judgmental with myself. I'm too hard on me.

# 5 What do you love about yourself?

That I am so free-spirited. That I am my own person. That I am secure in my being and what I came here to do.

That I know I am positive, and strong, and can get through hard times.

I love that I know how to turn my fire on when it's needed.

*"I want no separation between being a professional and being a priestess!"*

*Hadiiya*

Chapter six

# Jodi

Born: Kotelniki, Russia
50 Years Old

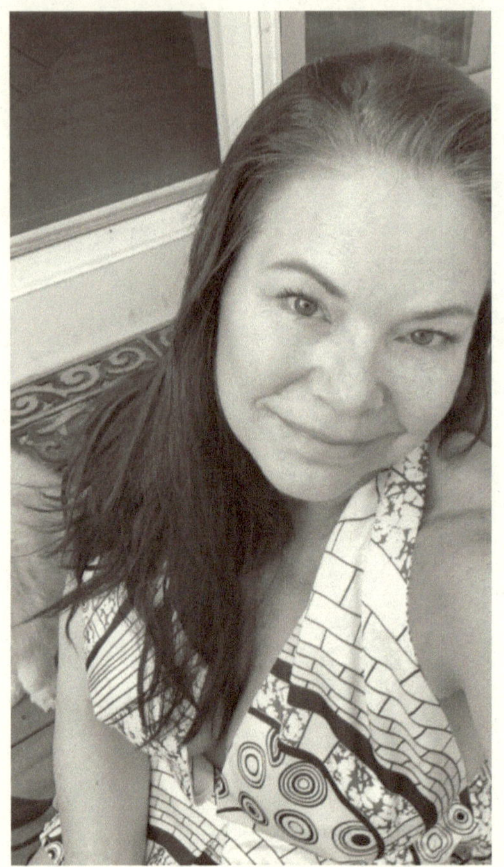

One day, driving by a building I've driven past a thousand times, I noticed a small sign for "Deep Tissue Massage". When I called the number, a woman answered the phone. For a moment, I was disappointed. I prefer a male masseuse because I've never met a woman strong enough to work out the kinks in my back. But when she said her name was Jodi, I changed my mind. The only Jodi I've ever met is in my novel, *Well-Behaved Woman Coming Undone.* I decided this was meant to be and made an appointment.

A few days later, I was there on her table in a warm room with soft lights. Jodi rubbed the side of my neck. "Somebody's been biting her tongue," she said.

How can this woman who doesn't know me — know me?

As if she has pressed a release button on my body, on my heart, I started crying. Big, gulping sobs. With her loving touch, Jodi gave me a safe space to acknowledge feelings I have been repressing for years.

I need this woman in my life.

When I asked her if I can interview her for this book on womanly wisdom, she said yes. I have a feeling Jodi says yes to life often.

We meet at Starbucks in the suburbs. Jodi comes in wearing yoga pants and a t-shirt, the uniform of middle-aged women everywhere. But there is no way you can confuse her with any other woman. With the mischievous twinkle in her eye and the earthly promise in the sway of her hips, she will undoubtedly lead you into trouble...

and somehow take care of you at the same time.

# 1 What would you tell your younger self?

Stop seducing your friend's Dads. I know you're not going to get caught, but that doesn't matter.

Not everyone who is messy is messed up.

I loved going to my friend Autumn's house. They were a mess and it showed. They sometimes lived in their car but they also had fresh vegetables. I lived in a perfect home that only had canned vegetables.

You're going to feel alone, most of the time. And that's okay. When you grow up, you can do things differently. And you will. You will become the healer you need now.

# 2 What would you tell your older self?

Oh, girl, you've lasted this long? Well played! I never thought I'd make it past thirty. I was going out young and fast.

Be a handful in the nursing home. I'd rather they say, "There goes Jodi", rather than "Jodi who?"

Keep believing in your Fairy tales, they've held you together this long. I am a damsel in distress and proud of it. It allows people to step up and be their best self. I can pick up a lawn mower and mow the lawn myself, but it's so much more fun to watch the boys do it.

I don't feel weak for needing people.

I never believe in the, "Girl, get up, no one is going to help you." It's incongruent with sisterhood.

You are never going to get younger, skinnier, or prettier than you are today. Enjoy where you are, in the body you've got.

# 3 What is most important to you right now?

If I'm going to be a Damsel in Distress, then I have to be able to give back, too. I am open to receiving help, but I am also very open to giving help.

Some of the Damsels I know are the best givers. They have the most to give because they know what it is to need help.

# 4 What do you struggle to accept about yourself?

I'm magic, but I know it's underutilized. Am I making a difference? What am I doing with my life and my gifts? Shouldn't I be doing more?

If it doesn't produce, my passion can wane. I'm a spiral-er. Either up. Or down. I have a danger of getting caught up in that.

I always feel like I'm getting away with something. All my life people have said to me, about me, "You're up to mischief." It's what people like about me.

And what they don't...

# 5 What do you love about yourself?

Everything!

I'm in love with myself every day. Wrinkles and pimples and dimples on my ass. I love my stretch marks, even though I hate them

I love that I fall in love with everything and anything a thousand times every day.

Be grateful, happy is a choice. I love that I can make that choice and have that power.

I'm good company with myself.

I'm having too much fun, too easy, too blessed. I know it's not that way for everyone.

My hubby brings me coffee in bed every morning. Sometimes he says, "I don't know what you did to deserve this?"

I smile like a cheshire cat. "Maybe I haven't done it yet."

*"When I was little, I wanted to grow up and be Dr. Ruth Westheimer. There was no shame in her game. I think her age and her looks gave her something I haven't inherently had.*

*I'm not bad, I'm just drawn this way!"*

*Jodi*

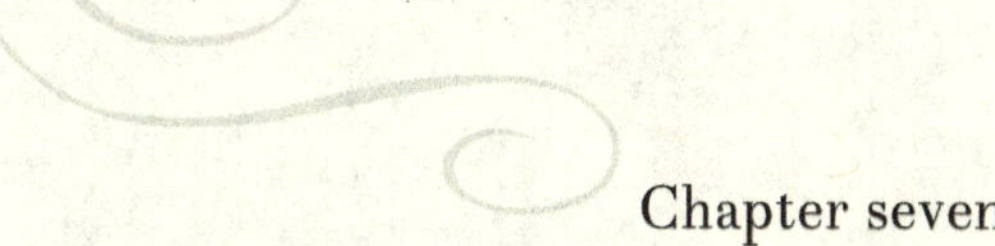

Chapter seven

# Charisse

Born: Santa Monica, California
63 Years Old

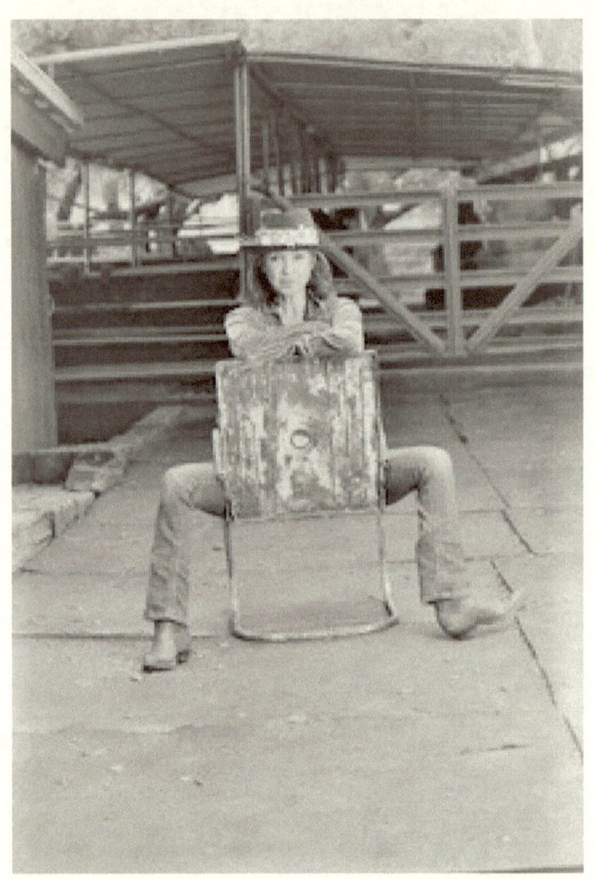

Letting go has been one of the lessons I've been struggling to learn for years. So when I find Charisse's website, TheLetGo, I invited her to be a guest on my podcast, The Writer's Block Podcast, NH.

During our conversation, she says something profound. "Most people think letting go means you will have less. But in letting go of things we don't need, we will actually have more."

She has hit the nail on the head of my own fear of letting go.

I pretend to ask the next question for our listeners, but truth is, my heart is clamoring for an answer. "Do you think most people are afraid if they let go, there won't be anything left under all the roles and identities they've worked so hard to become?"

"That's a good question." She sighs and repeats my words softly. "Afraid there won't be more."

Wait, to give her space to think and respond. I ask good questions of good women to get good answers.

Charisse does not disappoint.

"We are born enough," she says, "and we had nothing. Yet we were 100 percent enough. Then we start adding stuff on to weigh us down. In letting go, what we are really doing is taking away the excess of what is not needed to get back to the essence of being enough."

I want her to be my friend. My mentor.

Our sixty-something-year-old woman.

# 1 What would you tell your younger self?

I wish I understood forgiveness sooner.

My biological father was in and out of my whole life. When I was in my forties, I told him to never call me again.

When I was in my fifties, my cousin called me and told me he was dying.

"Hi, Dad."

He started in on me with his blame and victimization, but, I'm not playing this game anymore.

"You are dying," I said. "Is this the last conversation you want to have with me?"

Changing my reaction to him forced him to change his reaction to me.

"Hi, honey," he said. "How are you?"

For the first time in my life, I didn't need anything from him, I didn't need his approval, his support, I needed nothing. I could accept everything that brought us to this moment.

I cleared my eyes with forgiveness. I was able to see clearly, his spark, energy, philosophy. See who he was within me.

Up until that moment, I had been rejecting half my DNA. Forgiving him let me fall in love with all of me.

# 2 What would you tell your older self?

Keep your adventure bag packed.

Don't stop playing or being curious.

Find your own pacing. You don't have to go full out in everything you do. Take more time.

Be kinder to yourself.

I'm not looking for the outcome. I am looking for now.

# 3 What is most important to you right now?

I am learning to go with the current of life. Being kind makes me happy. It doesn't matter if something is going right or wrong, I can find something good.

I am not affronted by things like I used to be. I don't take things so personally. If something is not working, if a door is not opening, I sit for a moment. I still get frustrated, anxious and worried, but less. And less. And less.

Letting Go is the walk of my life, the talk of my life...

# 4 What do you struggle to accept about yourself?

I am too tough on myself.

I have an immense amount of patience for other people, but I am less patient with myself. I expect a lot.

The expecting is not the problem. Hardness is the problem.

In my journey to Om, the softness of yoga is helping me soften up on myself. The softest touch effects the biggest healing.

My yoga practice is slower, gentler, but deeper. We confuse soft with lazy and soft with easy, but softening is letting me go deeper.

And deep is hard!

# 5 What do you love about yourself?

My adaptability, my courage, and ability to change.

In my twenties, I wanted to be a writer.

Are you ready to be honest? I asked myself.

Of course I am!

NOT!

I realized when I was younger I was not ready to expose all of who I was because I was still learning who that was.

Now, there is not a single subject I can't talk about honestly. The things that embarrassed me when I was younger, my alcoholic father, my struggling mother, abortion... now I know there is nothing shameful about my truth. Or anyone else's.

There is nothing I am ashamed of. I learned to let go of shame as I matured.

But doing so readied me to speak my truth, in hopes that my stories could help others. It guided me to be compassionate about where they are. I can't stand on top of a mountain and say, "Hey, come up here!" I don't have that right...we are all on our journeys, but sometimes you need a hand...

I have to go down, meet them where they are, and say, "Let's walk up together." This is was what community does for each other, this is what strengthens society.

*"I love being a woman. Equality doesn't mean we're the same. The strength of a woman is not to be better than a man, but to bring to the table what a man cannot. Woman is more than man. Just look at the word."*

*Charisse*

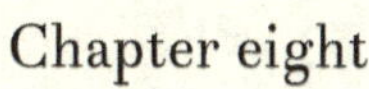

Chapter eight

# Carolyn

Born: Beals Island, Maine
79 Years Old

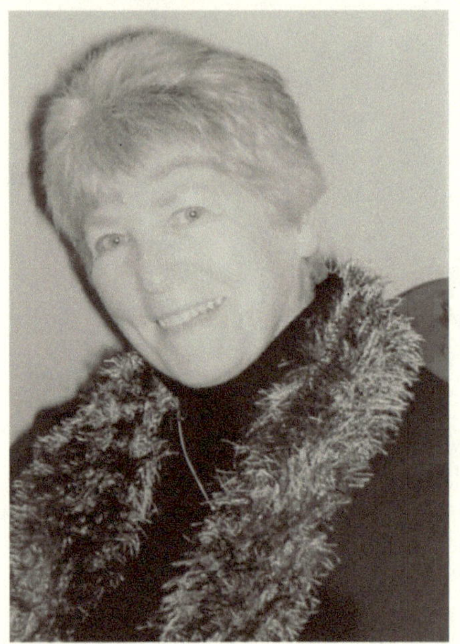

Finding a seventy-something-year- old woman has eluded me. I kept my eyes and heart open, but no one appeared.

A huge part of me knew this was resistance to finishing.

~~~~~~~

My Aunt had broken her hand and needed surgery. Her friend Carolyn was staying with her to take care of her. "She's the sister I always wanted," Aunt Cathleen said.

I felt a little tingle. "How old is Carolyn?" I asked, hopeful.

"Seventy-nine."

Of course she is.

I set up a time the following week for Carolyn and I to chat. Within moments, she mentions the Robert Frost poem, The Road Less Travelled. I have recently used that poem as a template to write my own poem, The Road Less Tango'd.

Shimmer, shimmer.
~~~~~~~

I told her I thought at fifty-five years old, I would be a knowledge cake, baked and cooling. Maybe there would be a little more frosting of learning, but overall, done.

"Honey, we never stop learning if we're open."

Carolyn broke my resistance, and I am forever grateful.

# 1 What would you tell your younger self?

I would tell her, I mean me, to enjoy things more in the present and not to be so into what's coming next that I miss what's happening now. I wish in my twenties I was more cognizant of how important each day is.

I would take the advice on the poster my Dad had hanging in his camp. It was a picture of an old, salty fisherman with his scruff beard, saying, "I have headman worries in my life. And most of them never happened."

# 2 What would you tell your older self?

Don't fear the future. Know that you are safe and secure and that heaven awaits.

Learn to trust God more and don't try to solve things by yourself. Ask for his guidance and help right away.

As I live each day, I need to live. . . each. . . day! Don't miss what each day can bring.

When I'm eighty-two or eighty-five, I will still be telling myself to do these things. I do them now, to a degree, but there are times when I deviate off the beaten path and I'd like to be doing it all the time. I don't want to waste a minute of this life and too often, we let time go by fussing and fuming.

# 3 What is most important to you right now?

The present.

# 4 What do you struggle to accept about yourself?

Choices I have made. I am still adjusting and accepting those choices. Choices that we make through life, major choices that we often make early on, change the direction of our life.

I love Robert Frost's poem, The Road Not Taken. I sometimes wonder if I had made this choice instead of the one I made, how would that change my life. Looking back, I'd like to have chosen the other road to see how it would have turned out. Do-overs would be rather interesting. I'm not fussing, but at this age, I often wonder, what if. . .

# 5 What do you love about yourself?

My name. . . Carolyn. It means "song of joy" and my Mom truly, rightfully named me.

*"Until I was eleven I was a tomboy. On Sundays, my mother dressed me up in frilly dresses and put bows in my hair, but the rest of the week, I was lobster fishing with my Dad, in hip rubber boots and my curls tucked under a baseball cap.*

*Then puberty hit and I found out what it was like to be a girl. I love being a woman. Guess I got the best of both worlds!"*

*Carolyn*

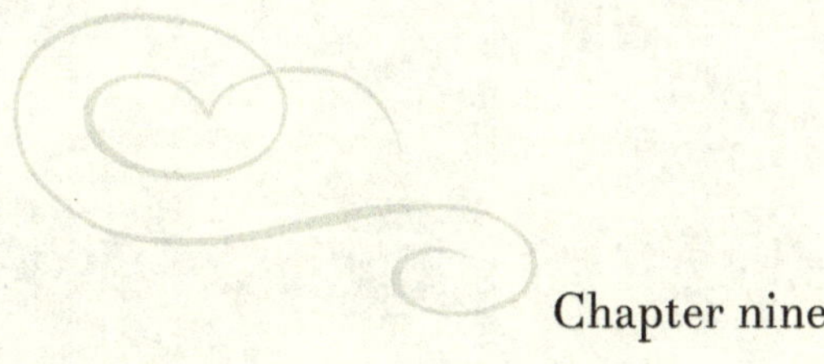

Chapter nine

# Nina

Born: Warsaw, Poland
89 Years Old

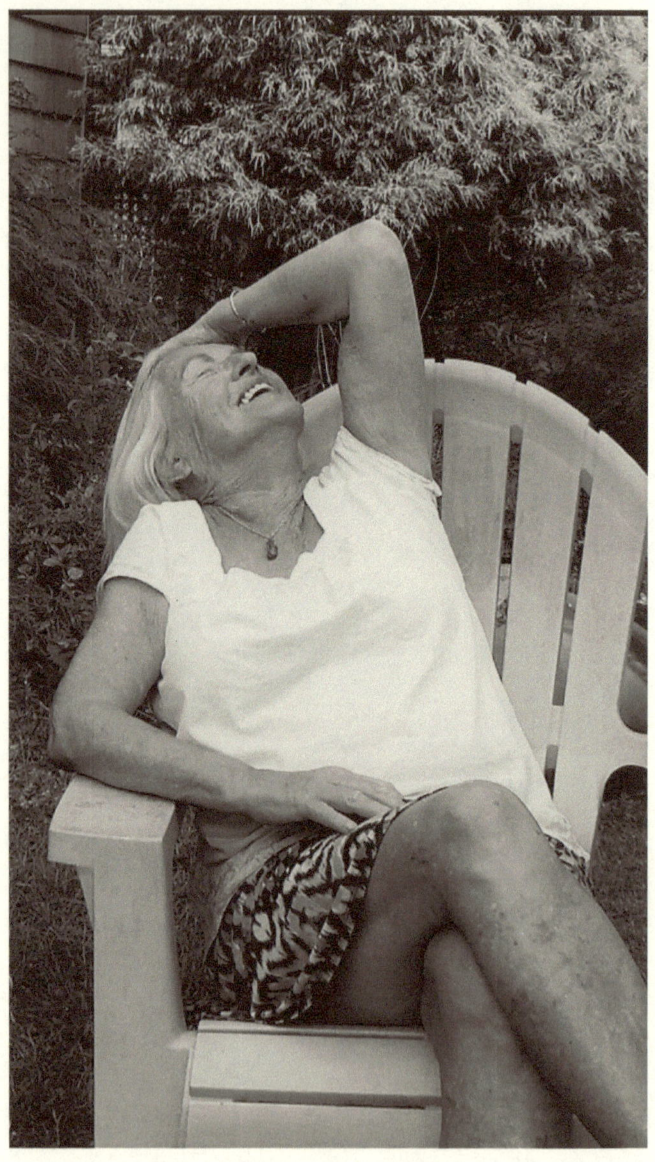

I was walking down the beach with Maureen, my best friend since sixth grade. Two women were sitting at the edge of the ocean in low beach chairs, their toes dancing in the waves. Maureen, an avid sewer, complimented the older woman who was wearing a beach dress with ruffles.

The younger woman explained that her mother, who was almost ninety, didn't speak English, so she translated. Her mother, Nina, smiled, got up from her low chair and did a little twirl.

We introduced ourselves. I heard myself tell them that I was a writer. And I was shocked that a second later, I started telling her about a project that has been in the back of my mind and bottom of my heart for a long time. "Someday, I am going to write a book about women of different generations. And I would like to have a picture of each woman in the book." Nina was so beautiful I asked if I could take her picture and have her contact information because I felt certain she was meant to be in this future project.

Nina stared into my eyes while Ava translated. Then she put her hand on her own heart, and then on mine. "Energy," she said with a heavy Polish accent, her hand going back and forth between our chests. Our hearts were connected.

I ran back to my blanket and got my phone and pencil and paper. As soon as I get home, I vow, I will make a folder and file this away for the future.

I am basking in the gift of the Universe speaking to me, through me. As I took a selfie with Nina, the world disappeared. Nina had a lilac scarf tied around her head and big sunglasses on, like a glamorous movie star.

Apparently, though, I was not listening close enough. Ava told me that Nina was going back to Poland in two weeks.

It was like the Universe slapped me on the back of the head to make me pay attention and get the whole message. . . I am not supposed to wait.

The Universe didn't care I was in the middle of finishing another book. Didn't care that I don't know any more about this project than what I told Nina. Apparently, through Nina, the Universe was telling me now. I needed to start this project now.

When the Universe speaks, I listen.

One week later, I am sitting in Ava's garden, with a huge bouquet of hydrangeas that Nina picked from her garden beside me, soaking up the sun and Nina's wisdom.

# 1 What would you tell your younger self?

Keep going. Maintain friendships. Keep a schedule so that on days you don't feel like getting up you have to get up and get going.

Connect with someone every day. Talk to someone. Don't be afraid to be alone, but try to have contact with other human beings every day. If your friends aren't available, go to the store or the bus station. Talk to strangers. Initiate a conversation with young people. And with old people.

Have something to look forward to. Having something to look forward to, a goal, is a gift.

Exercise your body. And your brain. And your heart.

# 2 What would you tell your older self?

Be as open and free as I am now. And listen to yourself.

When I was sixty, there was an older woman on the bus. She had the same name as my mother, and was born the same year, so she was the age my mother would have been. I stood up and gave her my seat. We talked for forty minutes. She told me one sentence, in Latin. Bloom at the spot God planted you.

It took me twenty years to place this sentiment in my life. It was hard for me to open, but gradually I did. I didn't get to be like this, she says with a flourish, until I was eighty. Wish I could have done it sooner.

# 3 What is most important to you right now?

Health. Both mental and physical. I am so thankful for my brain, grateful I haven't lost my interests. I exercise my body. I swim three times a week. In Poland, I have no need for a car because I can walk everywhere. I take gymnastic classes.

I exercise my brain as well. I keep up with the world. I read newspapers and keep up to date in the world.

Living bi-continental, six months in Poland and six months in the United States, I always have something to look forward to.

My friends ask, "Aren't you afraid to fly?" Doesn't even occur to me to be afraid. My world hasn't shrunk as I've aged. . . because I haven't let it.

# 4 What do you struggle to accept about yourself?

Too often, I stand in my childhood, still, after all these years. I was an observer of life, more than a participant. I never had guts. I was shy and insecure and I regret that I lost a lot. I didn't have friends. It always seemed like life was easier for other women. They would talk shopping and vacations and I just couldn't relate, I had none of that. I struggled, with two jobs, as a single mother.

I don't like to think about my past, sometimes. The unfinished business. With my sister. My ex-son-in-law. There were so many situations I didn't know how to deal with at the time. Now I know how I would handle things, but it's too late, and it haunts me.

My biggest regret, and sadness, is that life started after seventy. I am happier. More conscious. More present.

# 5 What do you love about yourself?

This new way of being open.

My whole life I felt overwhelmed and pushed down. When I was a child in Poland, I was sent to Russia during World War II. When I came back, we struggled. That's why I closed up. It took me a long time to learn how to take life on a lighter note and not stress about everything single thing. But I can finally be myself. I don't care what people say or think about me and I can talk about anything.

I was always scared, always afraid of becoming a grumpy old woman. I know plenty of them. Complaining old people, pessimistic at life. I refuse to become one of them.

*"In regards to men, it's important to know what to forgive, what to forget, and what to always remember. Contact with men requires wisdom of age. Younger women don't have that gift. That's why there are so many mistakes."*

*Nina*

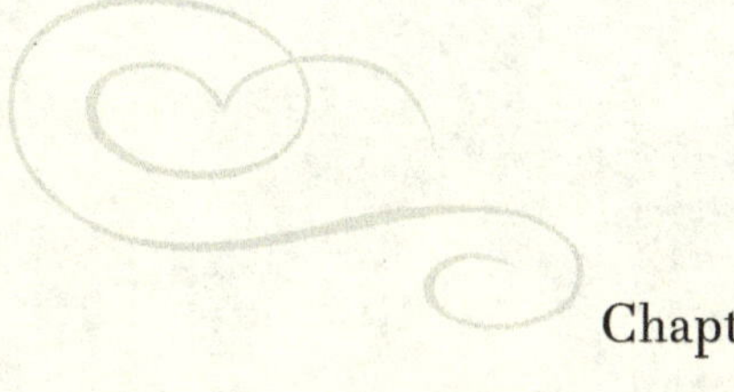

Chapter ten

# Frances

Born: Lawrence, Massachusetts
92 Years Old

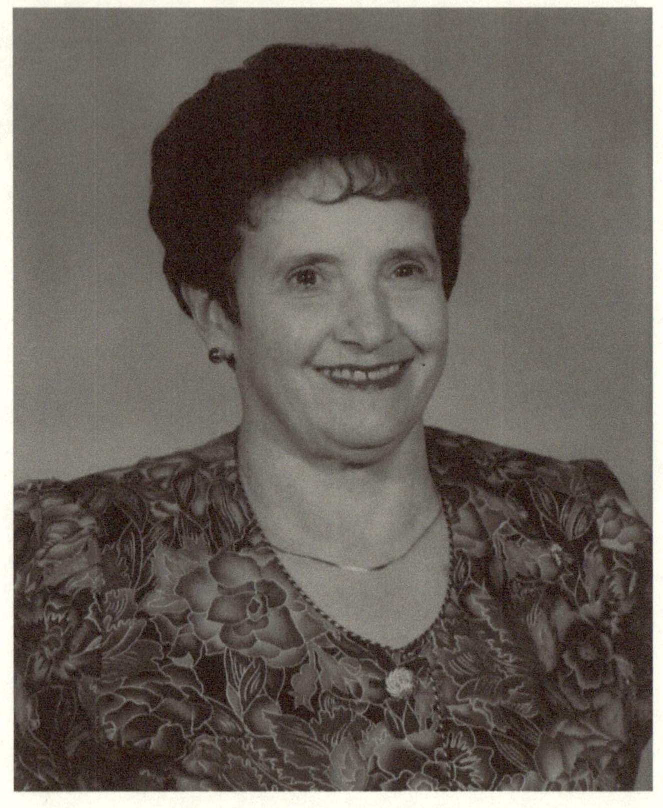

On a Tuesday morning, I was home by myself. I said, out loud to no one, "I don't know any ninety-something-year-old women,"

Wednesday morning, an acquaintance posted a picture of her mother, celebrating her ninety-second birthday. I called her and asked if I could set up a meeting with her mother.

A few days later, as I am leaving our interview, I ask Frances if I can hug her.

Her body is soft and her arms are cozy as they close around my body. There is no rush to this hug.

I cry all the way home, my heart breaking with memories of other hugs. . . I miss my grandmother!

And I realize my grandmother did something we modern women don't do. When I visited Nan, we would sit. And talk. And have a cup of tea. Black tea from the kettle on the stovetop that boiled in its own time. A happy whistle letting us know when it was ready. Then we would share our fortunes from the Lipton teabag. No instant Keurig with a million flavors, that are never as good as they sound, to pick from. No time to sit and chat and reminisce.

Women today are all so busy. We wear "busy" as a badge of honor. The busier we are, the more harried we are, the more important we must be. . . See what I'm doing. Not what I'm being.

This is a wisdom Frances has that too many of us have forgotten.

# 1 What would you tell your younger self?

Speak up. Tell my sister off. She was bossy and domineering. She had control of me. She was a year and a half older than me and I was too weak, and too quiet.

Then I would tell my sister-in-laws off. Right from the day I got married.

I never had trouble arguing with men. At work, even if they were my boss, I would speak up when they were wrong. And I would prove they were wrong.

So I guess it's women that I felt held me down. It was only years later that my other sisters told me my sister was mean to be because she was jealous of me. I looked like my mother and my mother was pretty.

# 2 What would you tell your older self?

I hope I can still walk.

I wish I could do what I used to do, but I can't. I use a walker now, but it's only for security. I can walk without it.

# 3 What is most important to you right now?

Being alive.

And seeing my grandchildren.

Being able to go out. My daughter comes once a week, she's my taxi driver now. We go to the hairdresser.

There's no such thing as family anymore. Every family I know is spread out all over the country. Because they're not near each other, they don't get together like we used to.

I remember one time when I got older, I told that sister who bullied me, "You go your way and I'll go mine."

That only lasted a few weeks because we were the only ones still living around here.

She's gone now.

## 4 What do you struggle to accept about yourself?

The thing I miss more than anything else is driving. I had my license when I was younger but my daughter jokes it was just for ID purposes. And to cash checks. Because we lived in the city, we had buses and taxis. We didn't own a car until my daughter needed one to get into Boston for college. When she graduated, we kept the car and my husband drove everywhere.

When he died in 1976, everyone in the family got all excited, wondering who I was going to give the car to.

No one! I had my license, and I had my car. I went and took a few driving lessons to freshen my memory. So I started driving myself when I was sixty-five. And I loved it.

That car gave me freedom. I didn't have to go far. I never wanted to go far. But I knew I could go wherever, and whenever, I wanted.

I think I was in my early eighties, when I couldn't pass the eye exam to renew my license.

# 5 What do you love about yourself?

That I'm ninety-two and I still live by myself in my own home.

That I have no regrets.

I have one friend left. She's ninety-five. She still works as an accountant. When her grandchildren ask her how old she is, she tells them she's thirty-nine. She's been thirty-nine for a really long time.

I am not lonely. I have my daughter. And my phone. \And my tablet. And my word puzzles. And my television. Sometimes I talk to it, and if it wants to talk back, I'm listening. It hasn't yet, but it might someday.

And I think my mind has stayed so sharp because I'm alone. I'm the only one I have to listen to. I don't have to listen to anybody else's problems. Or their arguments. Why would I want to do that?

And I'm still a good cook.

*"Really kind people end up taking in a lot of strays."*

*Frances*

Chapter eleven

# Eleanor

Born: Marlborough, Massachusetts
101 Years Old

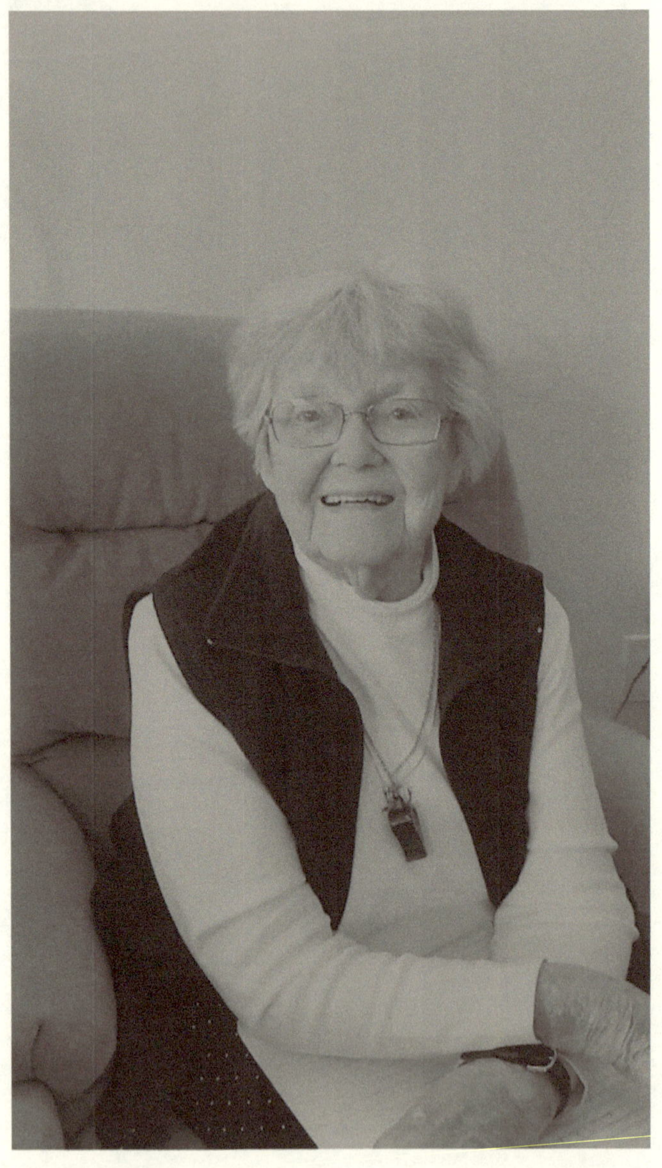

My Aunt told me about Eleanor, who is one hundred and one years old. In our conversation it came up that Eleanor's birthday is May 30. That's my birthday! There was the shimmer, the confirmation that she was the right woman.

When I meet her, Eleanor is waiting in the front room of the nursing home, a lovely parlor with thick rugs and dainty wallpaper. "Let's go to my room," she says, "so we can hear each other better."

With her clear blue eyes and her mischievous smile, she looks like the love child of Tinkerbell and the Keebler Elf. The ultimate hostess, she waits until I am seated before she sits down herself. She reaches over and pulls a photo album off the bookshelf beside her chair. She flips through until she finds the picture of the birthday cake her three children made for her last year. In bold red frosting, it says...

100 Years Loved.

# 1 What would you tell your younger self?

I am happy that I was able to attain so many friends growing up — and still today, keep in touch with their families.

# 2 What would you tell your older self?

Having celebrated my 100th birthday, I would tell my older self, be thankful for good health, education, good marriage and family.

# 3 What is most important to you right now?

Finding out what you're going to be writing.

I don't feel one hundred. I feel like I'm in my eighties.

Keeping able to teach and play card games. Enjoy visitors. And writing friends.

And, of course, the Red Sox!

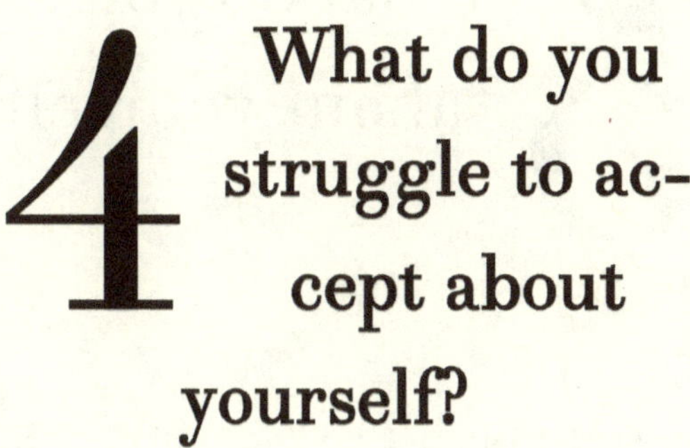

# 4 What do you struggle to accept about yourself?

Nothing.

# 5 What do you love about yourself?

That I can get up and walk and entertain. I have lots of company.

That I was able to give life to my family and so much love to them.

I love Frogs. You can see I have lots of them, ceramic ones on the shelf and on my dresser. Do you know what frogs stand for? she asks.

Fully Rely On God.

*"One holiday, I sat my kids down. I have something I want to tell you all together so one doesn't know before the others. A lot of my friend's kids are trying to take their parents license away. You will not need to do that. I am giving it up on my own. I think it's time. I've been driving since I was sixteen and I have decided I am done.*

*After all, I am ninety-six years old!"*

*Eleanor*

When we left Eleanor, Aunt Cathleen told me she had arranged for me to meet another woman. "She is one hundred and four years old and still lives in her own house."

"Interesting," I said, "but Eleanor was perfect. We have our ten women."

Then my Aunt told me the woman's name. Dorothy. My beloved grandmother's name.

I felt the shimmer in my bones. In the spirit of generosity, generosity of women and generosity of the Universe, I knew Dorothy needed to be included.

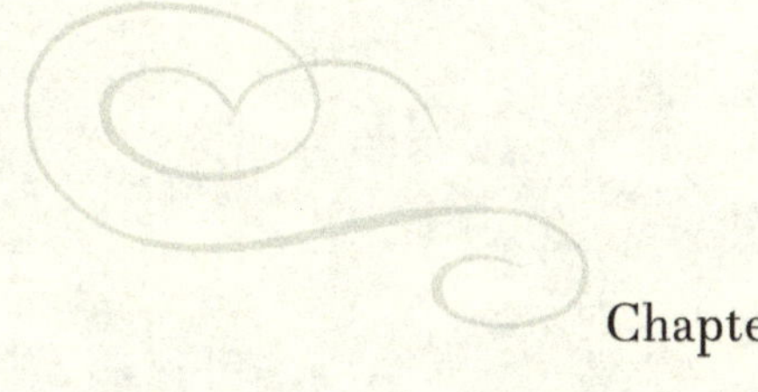

Chapter twelve

# Dorothy

Born: Eliot, Maine
104 Years Old

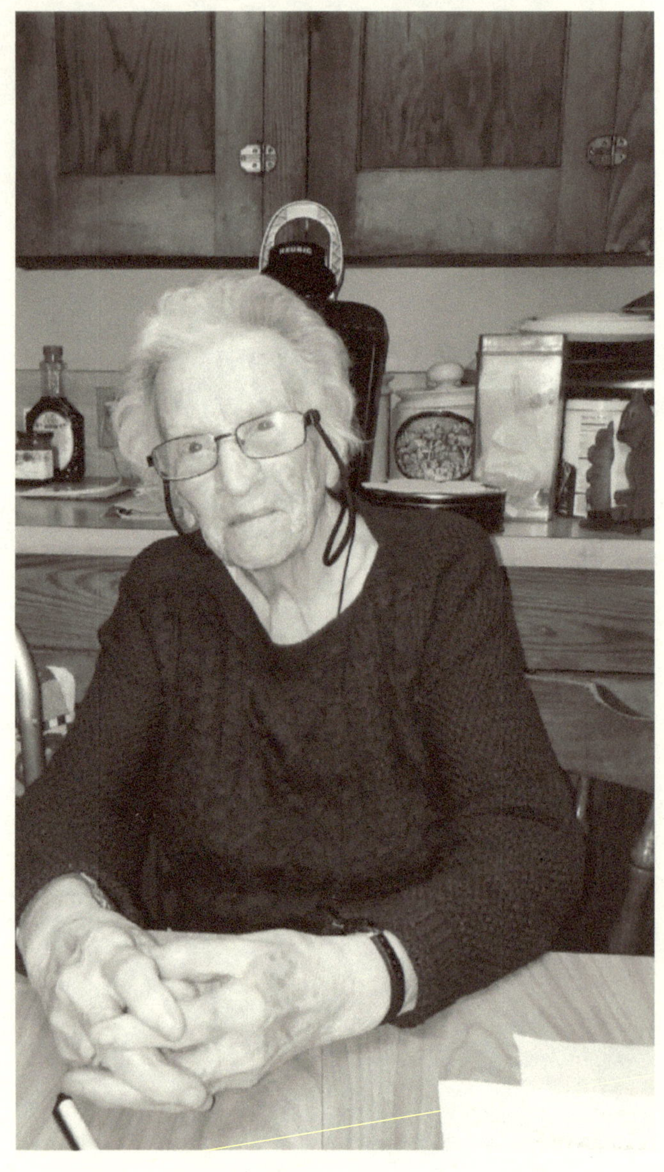

Sitting at Dorothy's wooden kitchen table, scratched from seventy years of family meals, I look at the chart on her wall, a big piece of construction paper with names and phone numbers written in colored markers. All people she can call and connect with when she needs to.

And Pam, from her church, is with us to make Dorothy feel more comfortable having me, a complete stranger, in her house.

"I still get my own breakfast," Dorothy says with a twinkle in her eye, "unless somebody takes me out to eat. And I have a woman who comes to my house to do my hair. We make a date, and she doesn't even charge me more."

We get distracted by scratching coming from inside the wall. "I heard squirrels last night," Dorothy says. "Think they got in through the attic. At first, I was afraid they might chew through the wall and eat me. Then it sounded like a whole family of squirrels," she says, "and I realized they just were trying to get warm."

For one moment, the idea of Dorothy lying in bed alone at night, with squirrels invading her home, makes me sad. I want to wrap her up in a blanket and take her home with me.

Then Pam goes into the other room and calls her husband. Within ten minutes, he arrives. He promises to capture the family of squirrels and release them back into the wild. I look down at the trap. Imprinted on the top are the words...

Have a heart.

Dorothy might have squirrels, but she is also surrounded by so much love that she doesn't need to go anywhere. She can live in her own home, exactly where she wants to be.

# 1 What would you tell your younger self?

I was born in Grandmother Spinney's house. I was premature so they put me in my grandmother's oven.

I am living proof that worrying doesn't shorten you life.

I wouldn't change anything..

# 2 What would you tell your older self?

Live while you can. Do what you can. And keep going!

Life is worth living as long as you try to do the best you can.

# 3 What is most important to you right now?

I am so thankful to have so many friends. Most of my relatives have gone before me. She points to a chart on her wall, written in colored markers, with the names and numbers of people she can call if she needs help.

I've lived here since 1940. My husband said we couldn't marry until he had saved some peanuts. Then he built this house, with our friend Bill Jenkins. He didn't charge us. That's just how people were in those days. And I've lived here ever since.

I enjoy life. I enjoy eating. I still get my own breakfast, unless someone takes me out for breakfast.

# 4 What do you struggle to accept about yourself?

I had two daughters. One of my daughters passed. No matter what people say, you never get over that. I know I never will.

# 5 What do you love about yourself?

I have kept a journal all my life. I just like to. It helps me to not worry.

Last night I had a bad dream I couldn't find my way home. I got up and sat in my chair. "Don't be silly," I told myself. "Get back in bed and go to bed."

And I did.

I seldom get blue like I used to. I just made up my mind. I don't think it's fun to cry, but I can cry and be happy.

*"The Lord wanted me here for this long. Maybe I'll find out why someday, and I'll yell down and let you know!"*

*Dorothy*

Chapter thirteen

# Me

It feels only fair that if I'm asking these questions, I should answer them.

# 1 What would you tell your younger self?

I wish I could have protected you better. I understand your desperate need for denial, but our greatest strengths are often our greatest weaknesses. Denial, which helped you survive a dark childhood, will haunt you and hurt you in your adult life.

Stop shining your light into dark places and people that keep the door closed and the lid on. It's not your fault they can't see the beauty that you see in the world.

I am sorry it took me so long to protect you, but I am learning and promise to do better. You survived with much of your light still intact. I am so proud of you!

# 2 What would you tell your older self?

Being needed doesn't mean being loved. I hope you haven't chickened out on learning this lesson. Those who taught you that need is the foundation of love didn't love you well. You deserved more.

I will love you. You might want more, hope for more, but I will love you enough that you won't need more.

# 3 What is most important to you right now?

Love.

I thought I knew what love was. I thought I loved a lot, and I thought I was loved a lot in return. I thought I needed someone to love. A mother. A brother. A husband.

I was wrong.

Needing someone else to love would mean that love is only available to me through another person. But love isn't a bridge of need between two people. Love isn't an excuse for bad behavior. It isn't something I need to chase, or find, or is anywhere outside of myself.

I am learning that love is an energy that comes from within — an infinite well that is available to me, always.

# 4 What do you struggle to accept about yourself?

That I am braver than I believe.

That I am enough on my own.

I didn't realize how much I have defined myself by my relationships. I am a good daughter if my mother says so. I am a good mother if my daughter is doing well and happy.

But what does that mean for me when Mom is upset or my daughter is struggling? I'm still trying to figure this out.

# 5 What do you love about yourself?

My soul-power to see potential.

And, I am re-claiming my imagination, the gift that came straight from heaven, because I believe imagination is meant to show us what can be.

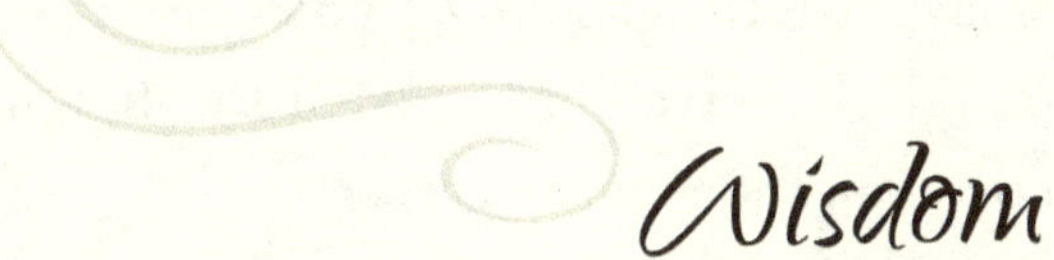

# Wisdom

...

I started this book with a tiny seed of faith that aging could be awesome.

I also had a bucket load of fear that I was wrong. That I was delusional. That my rose-colored glasses had finally blinded me to reality.

I wanted permission...permission to believe it was possible.

I wanted proof...proof that it existed in other women.

And most of all, I was desperate for an initiation.

Because the first two stages of being a woman I understood.

The path of the Maiden in my life had been clearly marked. Be good. Be quiet. Behave. Go to school. Get good grades. Go to college. Have some adventure, but not too much, then start a career.

The Mother role was also marked with clear instruction. Settle down. Be responsible. Nurture.

There was comfort in direction. In guidance. In the corralling. Safety in numbers and coloring inside the lines.

That statue of the Maiden, the Mother, and the Crone promised there was another phase of life that could take over when my time of mothering had passed. A hidden world, a secret garden for my own potential to take root and sprout. I imagined the path of the Crone would be illuminated with fairy lights. I would be given a purple velvet robe and walk barefoot through a gentle initiation into the wisdom my heart was craving.

Yet when it my time to be a Crone, I didn't have the faintest idea what that meant. I looked around and didn't see a lot of Goddesses dancing around their soul fire. I saw a lot of women meandering through the same life, year after year. I was a caterpillar inside the cocoon, terrified I didn't have the DNA code to transform into a butterfly, so I kept pretending to be who I had always been.

But the hands of time kept stripping me of identities I had spent a lifetime becoming.

Without a parent, am I still a daughter?

Without a young daughter, am I still mother?

Without driving ambition, am I still a career woman?

Letting go of the me I had spent a lifetime becoming has been agony, like a third- degree sunburn being peeled off my soul. I am glad I didn't realize this stripping was the first stepping stone on my personal Crone path, because I'm afraid if I could have refused this call, I would have.

Now that I have very little of the old me left to hide behind, I can sense the beauty of the blank slate, the welcoming embrace of emptiness. I have discovered that the path of the Crone is very different from the first two stages of being a woman. There is no well-worn path. No sign posts or road maps. Becoming a Crone is a solo journey. Choosing this route means I will have to forge my own path and make my own rules.

But that doesn't mean I am alone. The beautiful, incredible women in this book have proven that aging can be awesome. No longer a question, now a declaration — Aging can be awe-inspiring!

This book is a battle cry that aging is not simply the passage of time. It's about being brave enough to embrace every stage of the gift, and the burden, of being female.

For me, being a Crone means learning how to be a woman. Not a daughter, a sister, a wife, a mother, nor a friend.

Simply a woman.

Nothing more. Nothing less.

*Glorious!*

# Declaration of Wisdom

*If you can't say something nice about yourself...practice.*

*Believe you are enough. Always have been. Always will be.*

*Allow yourself to change. It's the only way to grow.*

*Connect with your intuition, knowing without knowing.*

*Let there be no shame in your game.*

*Let go of what no longer serves you.*

*A wise woman can lead, and follow, the dance.*

*Know the difference between what to forgive, what to forget. And what to always remember.*

*Be kind.*

*Be brave enough to choose your own path.*

*Heaven whispers...listen.*

*Imagination is meant to show us what can be.*

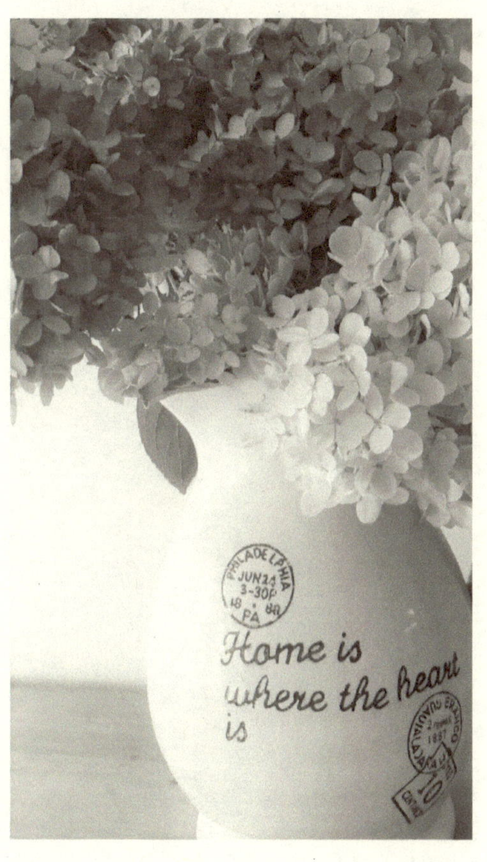


Hydrangeas from Nina's Garden

You can find the Declaration of Wisdom as
a hand-made greeting card, along with
Deborah's other books;

Searching for Julia Stone
Well-Behaved Woman Coming Undone
Storytime for Grown Up Women
The Wizard of MenopOz

in her Etsy shop;
DeborahMonkBooks.etsy.com

Place an order and write your favorite line
or best takeaway from The Wisdom of
Women in the notes,
and Deborah will include a free
autographed copy of this book to share the
wisdom with your favorite woman!

www.ingramcontent.com/pod-product-compliance
Lightning Source LLC
La Vergne TN
LVHW051001080826
845145LV00009B/2396